editora scipione

Presidência: Mario Ghio Júnior
Direção editorial: Lidiane Vivaldini Olo
Gerência editorial: Viviane Carpegiani
Gestão de área: Tatiany Renó
Edição: Luciana Nicoleti (coord.), Renato Malkov (coord.), Ana Lúcia Militello, Danuza Dias Gonçalves, Milena de Souza Rocha (assist.) e Natália Kessuani Bego Maurício
Planejamento e controle de produção: Flávio Matuguma, Juliana Batista, Felipe Nogueira e Juliana Gonçalves
Revisão: Hélia de Jesus Gonsaga (ger.), Kátia Scaff Marques (coord.), Rosângela Muricy (coord.), Brenda T. M. Morais, Carlos Eduardo Sigrist, Daniela Lima, Gabriela Macedo de Andrade, Heloísa Schiavo, Kátia S. Lopes Godoi, Luciana B. Azevedo, Luís M. Boa Nova, Luiz Gustavo Bazana, Patricia Cordeiro; Amanda T. Silva e Bárbara de M. Genereze (estagiárias)
Arte: Claudio Faustino (gestão), Erika Tiemi Yamauchi (coord.), Yong Lee Kim (edição de arte)
Diagramação: Lima estúdio gráfico
Iconografia e tratamento de imagem: Sílvio Kligin (ger.), Claudia Bertolazzi (coord.), Fernando Cambetas (pesquisa iconográfica), Fernanda Crevin (tratamento de imagens)
Licenciamento de conteúdos de terceiros: Roberta Bento (gerente), Jenis Oh (coord.), Liliane Rodrigues, Flávia Zambon e Raísa Maris Reina (analistas de licenciamento)
Ilustrações: Bruna Assis Brasil (Aberturas de unidade), Ari Nicolosi, Fabiana Salomão, Fabiana Shizue
Design: Gláucia Correa Koller (ger.), Talita Guedes da Silva (proj. gráfico e capa)
Ilustração de capa: Ideario Lab

Avenida Paulista, 901, 6º andar – Bela Vista
São Paulo – SP – CEP 01310-200
http://www.somoseducacao.com.br

Dados Internacionais de Catalogação na Publicação (CIP)

Morino, Eliete Canesi
Marcha criança : educação infantil : língua inglesa : 1 e 2 / Eliete Canesi Morino, Rita Brugin. -- 3. ed. -- São Paulo : Scipione, 2020.
(Coleção Marcha Criança ; vol. 1 e 2)

Bibliografia

1. Língua inglesa - Educação infantil I. Título II. Brugin, Rita III. Série

19-2855 CDD 372.65

Angélica Ilacqua - Bibliotecária - CRB-8/7057

2023
Código da obra CL 745858
CAE 720929 (AL) / 720930 (PR)
ISBN 9788547402617 (AL)
ISBN 9788547402624 (PR)
3ª edição
4ª impressão
De acordo com a BNCC.

Impressão e acabamento: Bercrom Gráfica e Editora

Uma publicação SOMOS EDUCAÇÃO

MARCHA CRIANÇA

A CAPA DESTE LIVRO PODE SER PERSONALIZADA PELA CRIANÇA DA MANEIRA COMO ELA QUISER. INCENTIVE ESTA ATIVIDADE. CERTAMENTE A TURMA VAI ADORAR!

EDUCAÇÃO INFANTIL

LÍNGUA INGLESA

2

ELIETE CANESI MORINO

Graduada em Língua e Literatura Inglesa e Tradução e Interpretação pela Pontifícia Universidade Católica de São Paulo (PUC-SP).
Especialização em Língua Inglesa pela International Bell School of London.
Pós-graduada em Metodologia da Língua Inglesa pela Faculdade de Tecnologia e Ciência (FTC-BA).
Atuou como professora da rede particular de ensino e em projetos comunitários.

RITA BRUGIN DE FARIA

Graduada pela Faculdade Superior de Arte Santa Marcelina (FASM-SP) e pela Faculdade Paulista de Artes (FPA).
Especialização em Língua Inglesa pela International Bell School of London.
Pós-graduada em Metodologia da Língua Inglesa pela Faculdade de Tecnologia e Ciência (FTC-BA).
Especialista em alfabetização, atuou como professora e coordenadora pedagógica das redes pública e particular de ensino.

MEU NOME: ....

MINHA TURMA: ....

APRESENTAÇÃO

QUERIDO ALUNO, QUERIDA ALUNA,

QUANTO MAIS CEDO COMEÇAMOS A ESTUDAR A LÍNGUA INGLESA, MAIS FÁCIL É APRENDÊ-LA!

COM A COLEÇÃO **MARCHA CRIANÇA**, VOCÊ VAI APRENDER DE MANEIRA DIVERTIDA, COM BRINCADEIRAS, CANÇÕES, JOGOS, CONTAÇÃO DE HISTÓRIAS, EXPERIMENTAÇÕES E OUTRAS ATIVIDADES.

TEMOS CERTEZA DE QUE VOCÊ VAI ADORAR ESTUDAR INGLÊS!

HAVE A NICE TIME!

AS AUTORAS

NAME: ....

....

CLASS: ....

CONHEÇA SEU LIVRO

VEJA A SEGUIR COMO SEU LIVRO ESTÁ ORGANIZADO.

UNIT

SEU LIVRO TEM QUATRO UNIDADES. EM CADA UMA DELAS VOCÊ VAI PARTICIPAR DE BRINCADEIRAS E INTERAGIR COM A TURMA.

LET'S SING!

AQUI VOCÊ ENCONTRA CANÇÕES SOBRE DIVERSOS TEMAS PARA OUVIR E CANTAR COM OS COLEGAS E O PROFESSOR.

IT'S YOUR TURN!

VOCÊ TAMBÉM VAI PARTICIPAR DE ATIVIDADES DE EXPERIMENTAÇÃO, EXPLORAR TEMAS IMPORTANTES E VIVENCIAR NOVAS PRÁTICAS.

LESSON

EM CADA UNIDADE HÁ TRÊS LIÇÕES COM VOCABULÁRIO NOVO, CONTAÇÃO DE HISTÓRIAS E ATIVIDADES VARIADAS.

TALKING ABOUT

VOCÊ VAI CONTAR E OUVIR HISTÓRIAS, REALIZAR ATIVIDADES E DISCUTIR IDEIAS COM OS COLEGAS, REFLETINDO SOBRE TEMAS ATUAIS.

GLOSSARY

AQUI VOCÊ ENCONTRA UM GLOSSÁRIO ILUSTRADO COM AS PALAVRAS ESTUDADAS AO LONGO DO LIVRO.

MATERIAL COMPLEMENTAR

HOLIDAY CARDS
CARTÕES DE DATAS COMEMORATIVAS

MEMORY GAME
JOGO DA MEMÓRIA

READER
LET'S MAKE POPCORN

DOMINOES
DOMINÓ

STICKERS
ADESIVOS

ÍCONES

LISTEN · MATCH · CIRCLE · NUMBER · MAKE AN X · SAY · STICK

COLOR · DRAW · COUNT · DOT TO DOT · POINT · PRESS OUT · STORYTELLING

CONTENTS

Bruna Assis Brasil/Arquivo da editora

UNIT 1 NATURE

LET'S PLAY! PLEASE, MR. CROCODILE!

Bruna Assis Brasil/Arquivo da editora

PETS

① LOOK, LISTEN AND SAY. 2

DATE ....../....../......

② COLOR AND SAY.

Ilustrações: Ari Nicolosi/Arquivo da editora

DATE ___ / ___ / ___

3 CIRCLE THE ODD ONE OUT.

Ilustrações: Ari Nicolosi/Arquivo da editora

DATE ____ / ____ / ____

4 MAKE AN **X** AND COLOR.

Ilustrações: mhatzapa/Shutterstock

DATE ____ / ____ / ____

5 LOOK, COUNT AND COLOR.

5

2

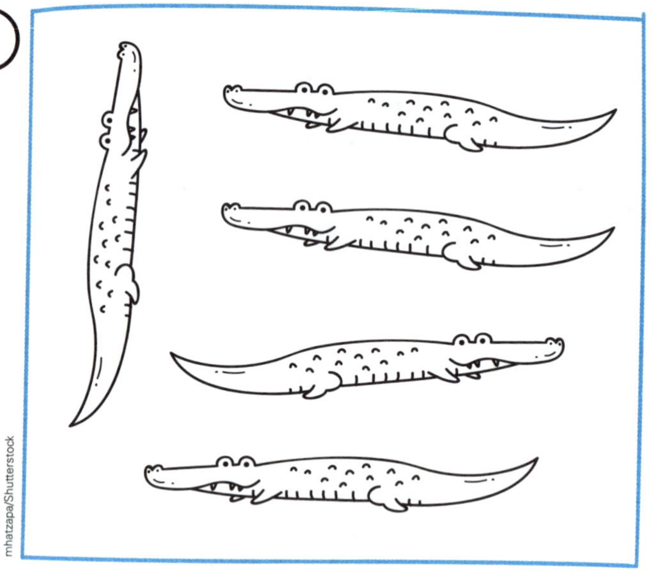

3

4

1

DATE ____ / ____ / ____

LET'S SING! 3

DOGS AND CATS

DOGS AND CATS,
DOGS AND CATS,
DOGS: BOW-WOW!
CATS: MEOW! MEOW!
I LOVE DOGS,
I LOVE CATS,
LOVELY PETS!
LOVELY PETS!

Ari Nicolosi/Arquivo da editora

Tartila/Shutterstock

DATE ___/___/___

LESSON 2

FARM ANIMALS

1 LOOK, LISTEN AND SAY. 4

DATE ...... / ...... / ......

2 LISTEN AND CIRCLE THE ANIMALS.

DATE ____ / ____ / ____

③ MATCH AND SAY.

Nerthuz/Shutterstock

Eric Isselee/Shutterstock

photomaster/Shutterstock

Tsekhmister/Shutterstock

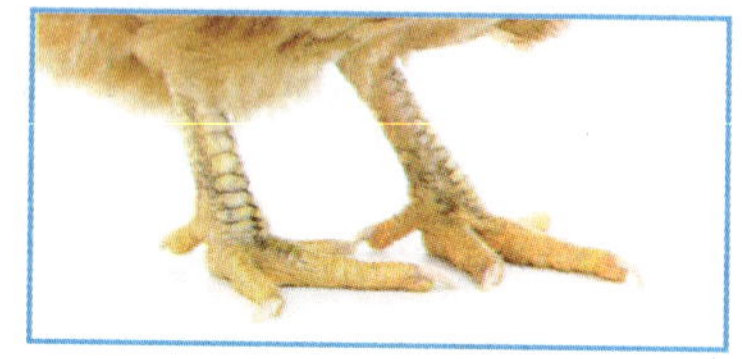

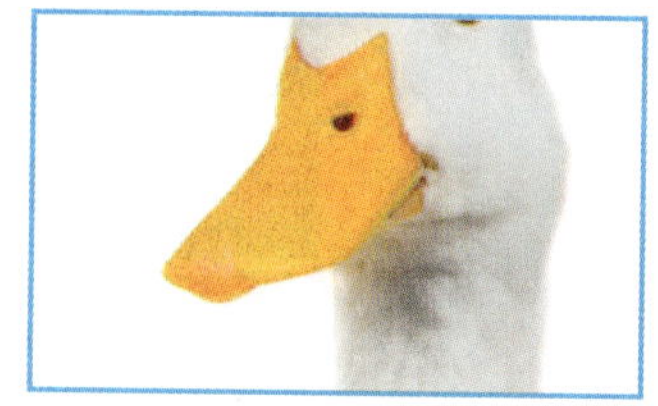

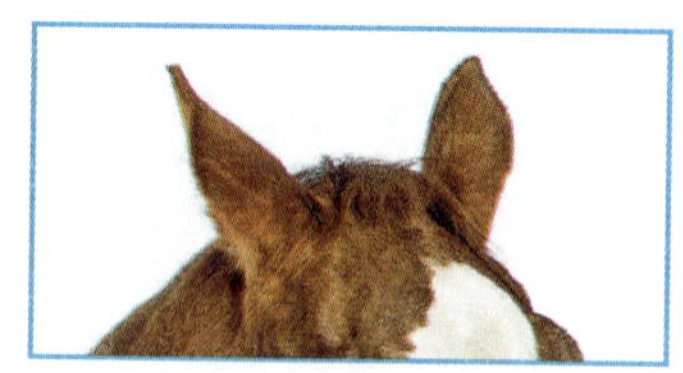

DATE ____ / ____ / ____

4 FIND THE WAY.

Klara Viskova/Shutterstock

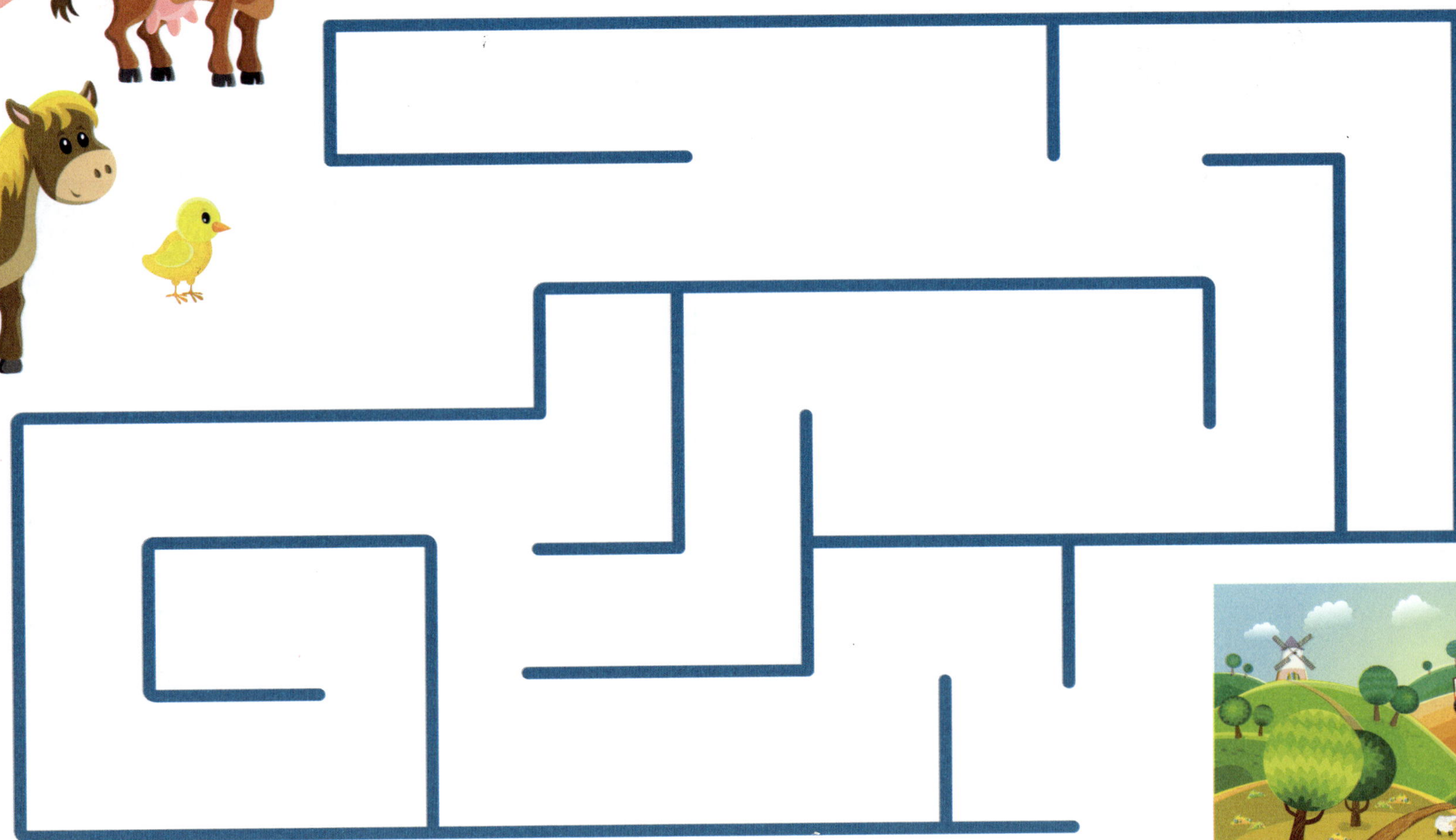

Denis Demidenko/Shutterstock

DATE ..../......../........

5 STICK.

PETS	FARM ANIMALS

DATE ____ / ____ / ____

LET'S SING! 5

THE ANIMALS ON THE FARM

THE COWS ON THE FARM MOO ALL THE TIME
ALL THE TIME, ALL THE TIME.
THE COWS ON THE FARM DO IT ALL THE TIME
THEY GO MOO-MOO!

THE HORSES ON THE FARM NEIGH ALL THE TIME
ALL THE TIME, ALL THE TIME,
THE HORSES ON THE FARM NEIGH ALL THE TIME
THEY GO NEIGH, NEIGH!

THE PIGS ON THE FARM GRUNT ALL THE TIME
ALL THE TIME, ALL THE TIME!
THE PIGS ON THE FARM GRUNT ALL THE TIME
THEY GO OINK, OINK!

THE CHICKENS ON THE FARM CLUCK ALL THE TIME
ALL THE TIME, ALL THE TIME!
THE CHICKENS ON THE FARM CLUCK ALL THE TIME
THEY GO CLUCK, CLUCK!

MOO-MOO! NEIGH, NEIGH!
OINK, OINK! CLUCK, CLUCK!
THEY DO IT ALL THE TIME! (REPEAT)

DATE .... / .... / ....

LESSON 3

AT THE PARK

1 LOOK, LISTEN AND SAY. 6

Ari Nicolosi/Arquivo da editora

DATE .... / .... / ....

2 LISTEN AND COLOR.

DATE ____ / ____ / ____

3 LOOK AND CIRCLE.

Ilustrações: Ari Nicolos/Arquivo da editora

DATE ____ / ____ / ____

4 COMPLETE AND COLOR.

Ilustrações: Ari Nicolosi/Arquivo da editora

5 LOOK AND DRAW.

OUR WALK IN NATURE!

I SEE...

I SMELL...

I FEEL...

I HEAR...

DATE ____/____/____

LET'S SING!

7

A CAT IN THE TREE

LOOK! A PINK FLOWER!
LOOK! LOOK! A BIG TREE!
LOOK, A YELLOW BIRD!
LOOK! LOOK, A CAT IN THE TREE.

OH! A CAT IN THE TREE?
YES, A CAT IN THE TREE...
AND A BIRD IN THE TREE.
IT'S WHAT YOU SEE!
MEOW! MEOW!
TWEET! TWEET!

Ari Nicolosi/Arquivo da editora

DATE ____/____/____

TALKING ABOUT

CONSERVATION

1. LOOK AND TELL A STORY.

Ilustrações: Fabiana Shizue/Arquivo da editora

DATE ____ / ____ / ____

UNIT 2 THE CITY

LET'S PLAY! RED LIGHT, GREEN LIGHT

Bruna Assis Brasil/Arquivo da editora

MEANS OF TRANSPORTATION

1 LOOK, LISTEN AND SAY. 8

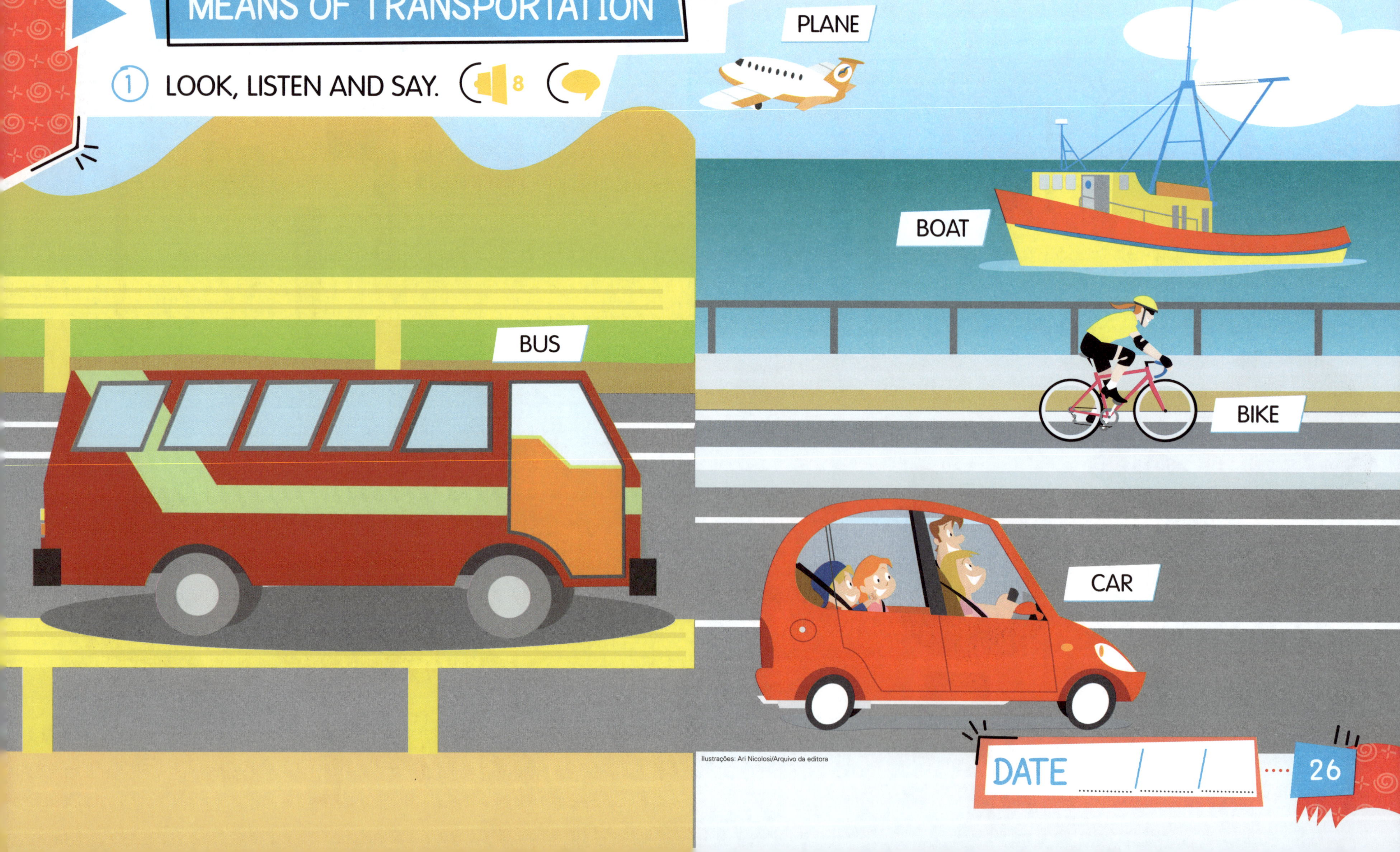

Ilustrações: Ari Nicolosi/Arquivo da editora

DATE .... / .... / ....

2 LISTEN AND NUMBER THE SEQUENCE.

Ari Nicolosi/Arquivo da editora

DATE ..... / ..... / .....

3 MATCH.

DATE ____ / ____ / ____

④ LOOK AND DRAW.

irysha/Shutterstock

inacioluc/Shutterstock

Thomas Fredriksen/Shutterstock

DATE ____/____/____

5 STICK.

DATE ___/___/___

LET'S SING! 9

I GO BY...

YadvigaGr/Shutterstock

GO BY...

BY CAR,
BY BUS,
BY PLANE.
I GO BY CAR,
BEEP, BEEP!
I GO BY BUS,
BRUUUMM!
I GO BY PLANE,
ZZOOMM!

BY CAR,
BY BUS,
BY PLANE.
BY CAR,
BY BUS,
BY PLANE.

DATE ____/____/____

LESSON 5

PLACES IN THE CITY

1 LOOK, LISTEN AND SAY. 10

Ari Nicolosi/Arquivo da editora

DATE .... / .... / ....

② LISTEN AND MAKE AN **X**.

Ari Nicolosi/Arquivo da editora

DATE ____ / ____ / ____

3 CIRCLE THE ODD ONE OUT.

Ilustrações: Ari Nicolosi/Arquivo da editora

Vladislav Kudoyarov/Shutterstock

DATE ____/____/____

4 MATCH.

Gary Hider Photography/Shutterstock

SUPERMARKET

Lance Huntress/Shutterstock

HOSPITAL

Lester Balajadia/Shutterstock

PET SHOP

Piotr Wytrazek/Shutterstock

SCHOOL

ang intaravichian/Shutterstock

BOOK

Eric Isselee/Shutterstock

DOG

natrot/Shutterstock

ECOBAG

Hugo1989/Shutterstock

AMBULANCE

DATE .... / .... / ....

5 LOOK AND COLOR.

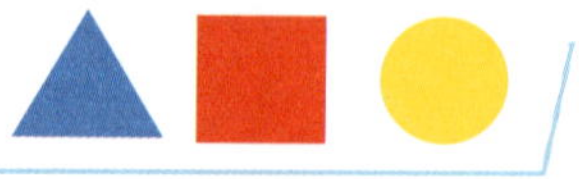

Ari Nicolosi/Arquivo da editora

DATE ____ / ____ / ____

LET'S SING! 11

WHAT A BUSY DAY!

WHAT A BUSY DAY!
WHAT A BUSY DAY!
MANY PLACES TO GO
MANY THINGS TO DO

GO TO SCHOOL
GO TO THE PET SHOP
GO TO THE HOSPITAL
GO TO THE SUPERMARKET

MANY PLACES TO GO
MANY THINGS TO DO
WHAT A BUSY DAY!
WHAT A BUSY DAY!

DATE ...../...../.....

LESSON 6

COLORS AND NUMBERS

① LOOK, LISTEN AND SAY. 12

Ari Nicolosi/Arquivo da editora

RED

PINK

YELLOW

GREEN

ORANGE

BLUE

DATE ..... / ..... / .....

② LOOK, LISTEN AND SAY. 13

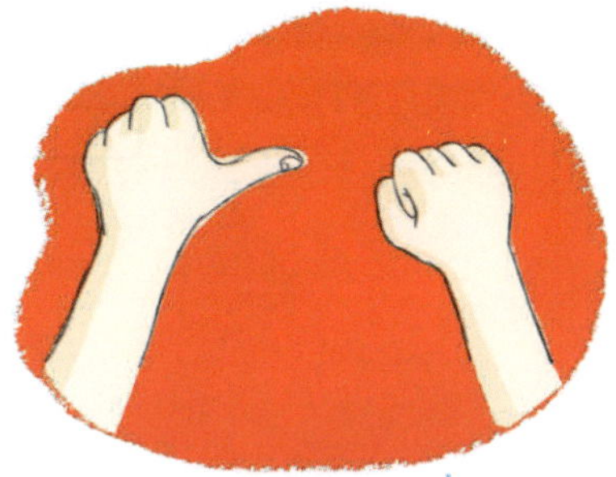
1 • ONE

2 • TWO

Ilustrações: Fabiana Salomão/Arquivo da editora

3 • THREE

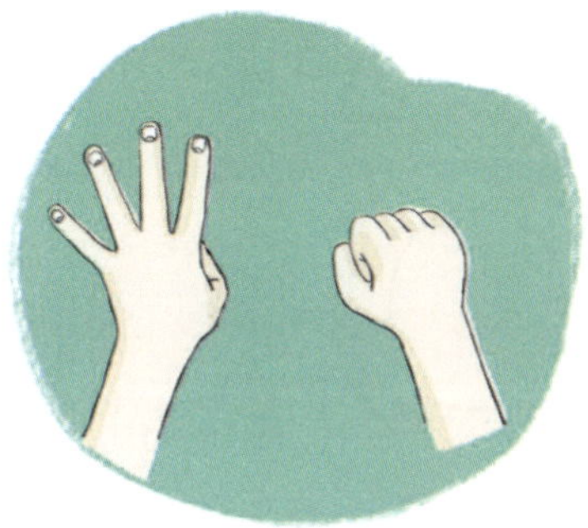
4 • FOUR

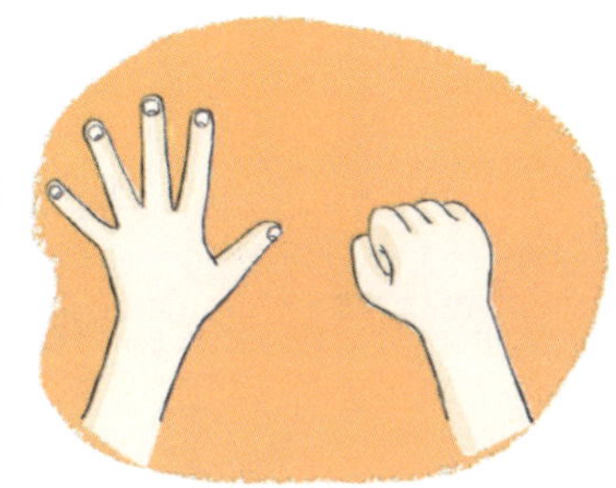
5 • FIVE

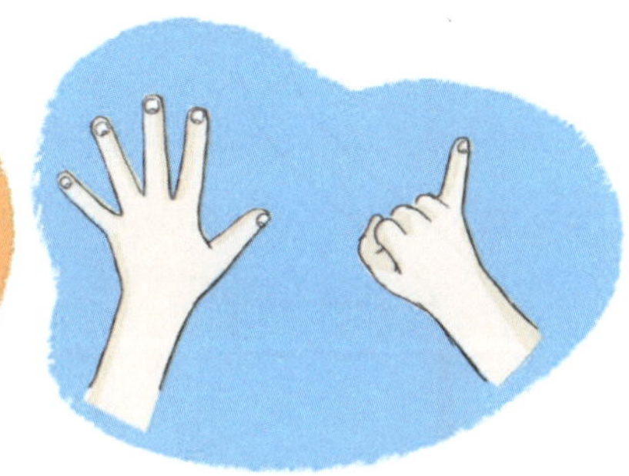
6 • SIX

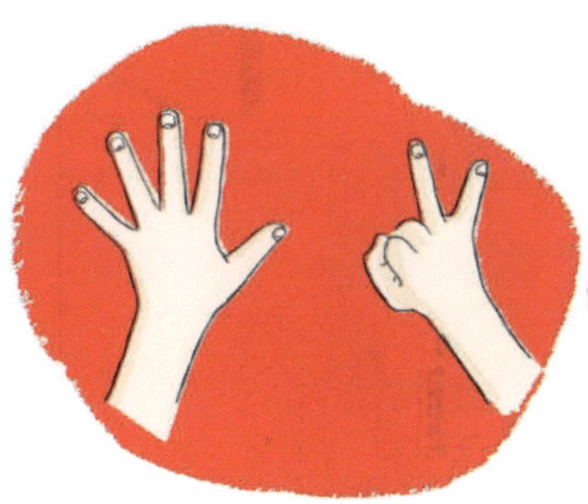
7 • SEVEN

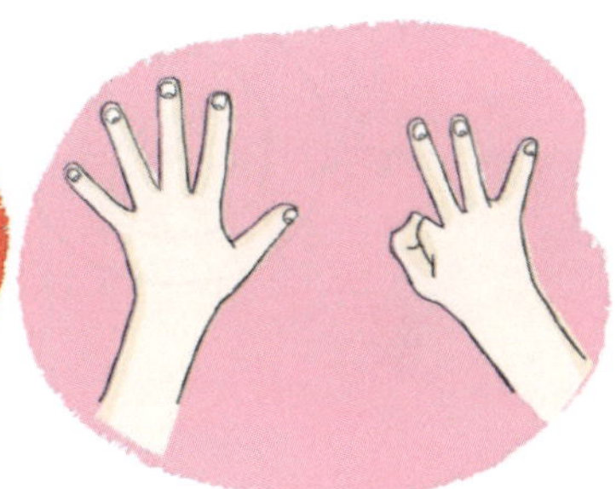
8 • EIGHT

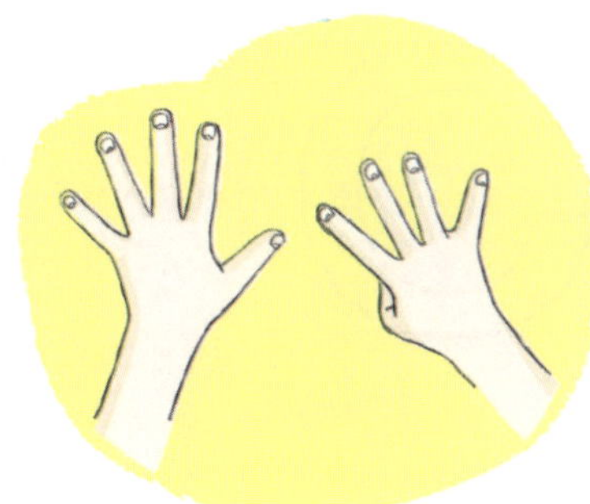
9 • NINE

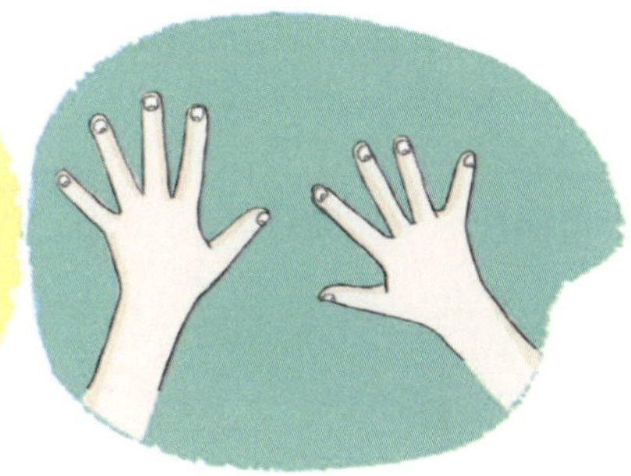
10 • TEN

DATE ____/____/____

3 LISTEN AND COLOR.

1 3 7

2 6 9

4 5 8 10

4 COUNT AND NUMBER.

PLANE

ifong/Shutterstock

BIKE

Gilang Prihardono/Shutterstock

SCHOOL

MAVRITSINA IRINA/Shutterstock

PET SHOP

Barry Barnes/Shutterstock

5 COLOR.

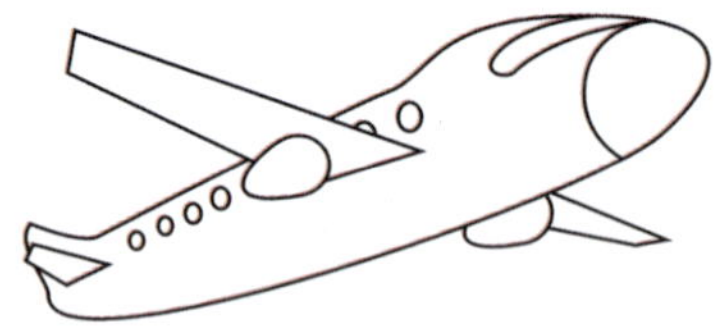

Ari Nicolosi/Arquivo da editora

DATE ___ / ___ / ___

LET'S SING!

14

SHOW ME THE COLORS

SHOW ME ONE RED BALL!
YES: RED! ONE RED BALL!
SHOW ME TWO YELLOW BALLS!
YES: YELLOW! TWO YELLOW BALLS!

SHOW ME THREE GREEN BALLS!
YES: GREEN! THREE GREEN BALLS!
SHOW ME FOUR BLUE BALLS!
YES: BLUE! FOUR BLUE BALLS!

SHOW ME ALL THE COLORS!
RED, YELLOW, GREEN, BLUE!
YES: ALL THE COLORS!
RED, YELLOW, GREEN, BLUE!

ayelet-keshet/Shutterstock

DATE ____/____/____

IT'S YOUR TURN!

LET'S MAKE AN ART EXHIBITION!

① LOOK AND SAY.

O MAMOEIRO, TARSILA DO AMARAL, 1925.

② COLOR.

DATE .... / .... / ....

UNIT 3 THE HUMAN BODY

LET'S PLAY! SIMON SAYS...

Bruna Assis Brasil/Arquivo da editora

MY BODY

1 LOOK, LISTEN AND SAY. 15

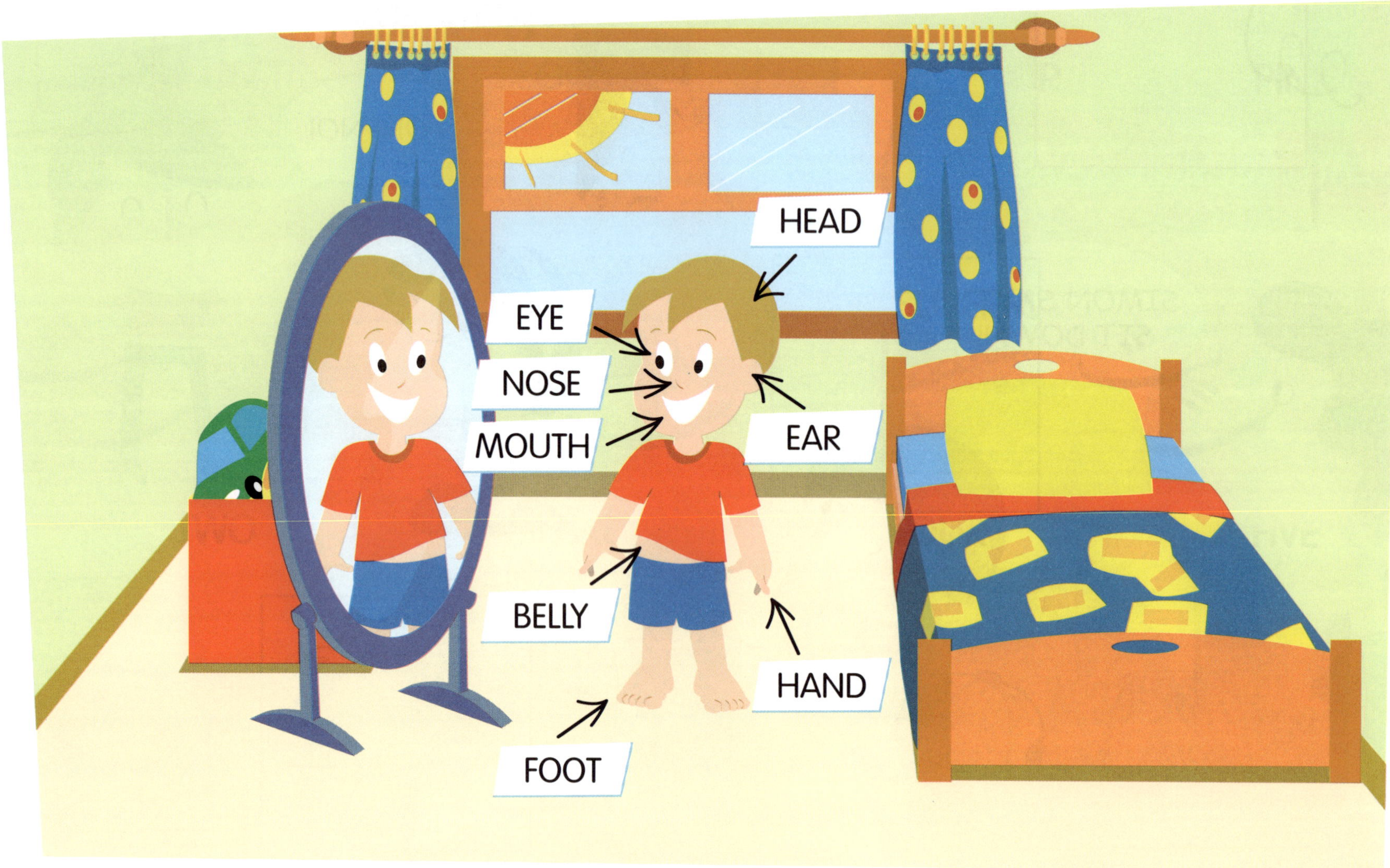

Ari Nicolosi/Arquivo da editora

DATE ____ / ____ / ____

② LISTEN AND CIRCLE.

DATE .... / .... / ....

③ LOOK, FIND AND CIRCLE.

2 NOSES   4 MOUTHS   6 EARS   8 EYES

DATE ____ / ____ / ____

4 MATCH.

ANURAK PONGPATIMET/Shutterstock

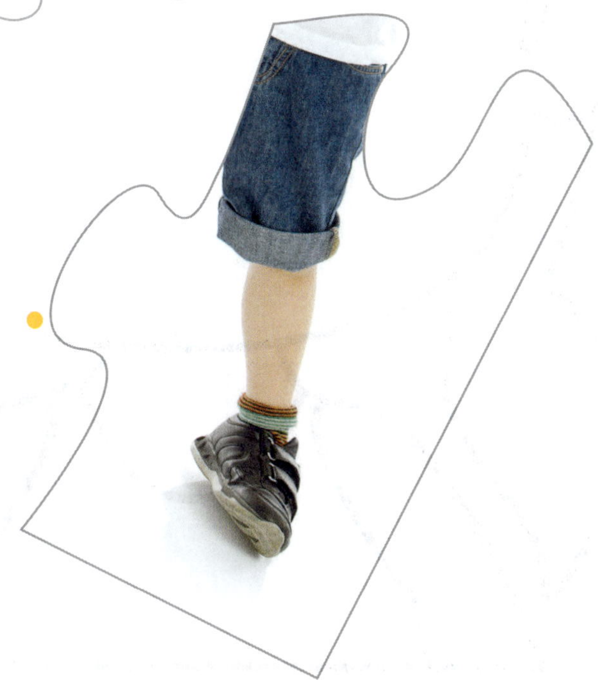

DATE ..../........./.........

5 DRAW, COLOR AND SAY.

DATE ____/____/____

LET'S SING! 16

HAND AND FOOT

SHOW ME A HAND,
SHOW ME A HAND,
WAVE THE HAND!
HELLO! HELLO!
SHOW ME YOUR FOOT,
SHOW ME YOUR FOOT,
STAMP YOUR FOOT!
POW, POW!
HAND, HAND!
FOOT, FOOT!
HELLO, HELLO!
POW, POW!

Ilustrações: Fabiana Salomão/Arquivo da editora

DATE ____/____/____

LESSON 8

BODY CARE

1 LOOK, LISTEN AND SAY. 17

An Nicolosi/Arquivo da editora

BRUSH YOUR TEETH

COMB YOUR HAIR

TAKE A SHOWER

WASH YOUR HANDS

DATE .... / .... / ....

② LISTEN AND NUMBER.

Ilustrações: Ari Nicolosi/Arquivo da editora

DATE ____ / ____ / ____

③ LOOK AND NUMBER.

① 

②

③ 

Ilustrações: Ari Nicolos/Arquivo da editora

DATE .... / .... / ....

4 CIRCLE THE ODD ONE OUT.

Raul Mellado Ortiz/Shutterstock

NetPhotographer/Shutterstock

Ann in the uk/Shutterstock

Porvata Tripper/Shutterstock

HappyChildren/Shutterstock

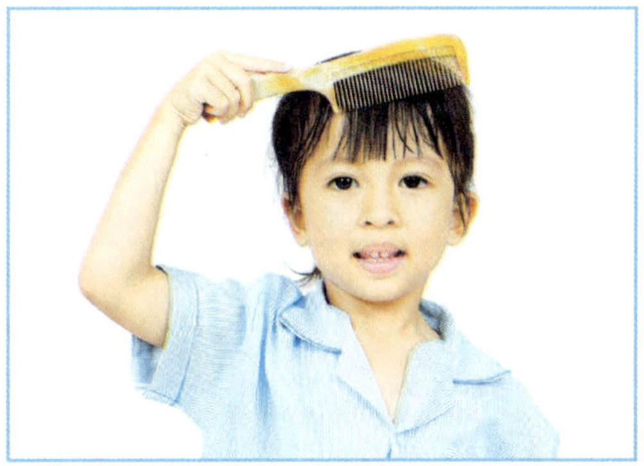

TOM...foto/Shutterstock

pitsanu suanlim/Shutterstock

Khosro/Shutterstock

didesign021/Shutterstock

Magomed Magomedagaev/Shutterstock

Aaron Amat/Shutterstock

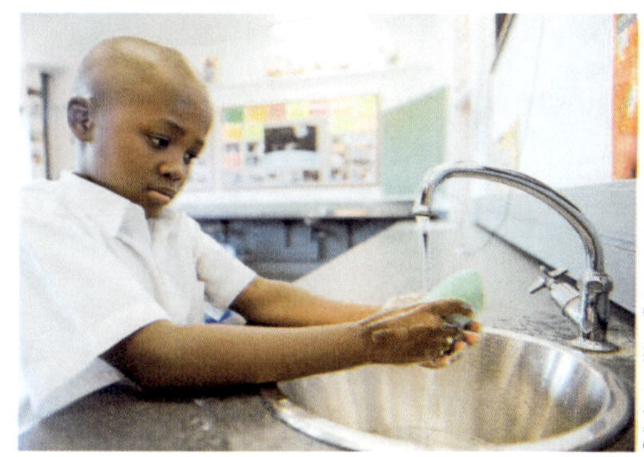

Gallo Images/Alamy/Fotoarena

DATE .... / .... / ....

5 CIRCLE 4 DIFFERENCES.

Ilustrações: Ari Nicolosi/Arquivo da editora

DATE ..../........../..........

LET'S SING! 18

Lorelyn Medina/Shutterstock

BODY CARE, BODY CARE

BRUSH YOUR TEETH,
COMB YOUR HAIR,
WASH YOUR HANDS
AND TAKE A SHOWER.
TAKE A SHOWER!

BODY CARE, BODY CARE
BODY, BODY, BODY CARE!

DATE .... / .... / ....

LESSON 9

MY CLOTHES

1 LOOK, LISTEN AND SAY. 19

Ilustrações: Ari Nicolosi/Arquivo da editora

DATE ..../......../........

② CIRCLE THE MISSING CLOTHES.

Ilustrações: Ari Nicolosi/Arquivo da editora

DATE ____ / ____ / ____

3 STICK.

DATE ___ / ___ / ___

4 MATCH.

JFCfotografic/Shutterstock

vetasster/Shutterstock

Irina Rogova/Shutterstock

MK photograp55/Shutterstock

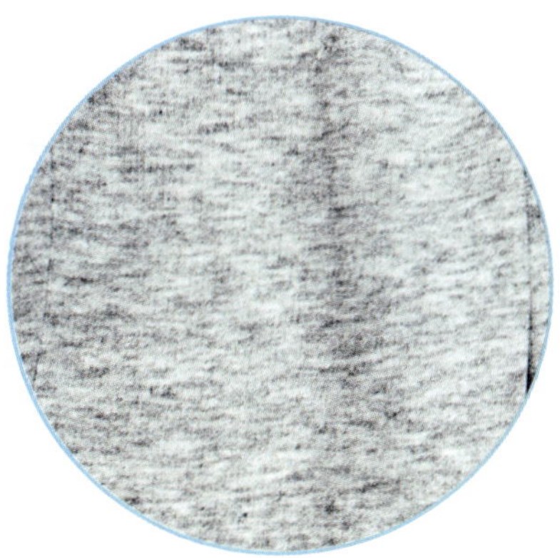

DATE ____/____/____

5 DRAW AND COMPLETE THE SEQUENCE.

DATE ____ / ____ / ____

LET'S SING!

20

DRESS UP!

PUT ON YOUR T-SHIRT!
PUT ON YOUR SHORTS!
PUT ON YOUR SOCKS!
PUT ON YOUR SHOES!
HURRY UP! HURRY UP!
YOU ARE LATE FOR SCHOOL!

Lorelyn Medina/Shutterstock

DATE ____/____/____

TALKING ABOUT

SELF-CARE

1 LOOK AND TELL A STORY.

Ilustrações: Fabiana Shizue/Arquivo da editora

DATE ____ / ____ / ____

UNIT 4 FOOD

LET'S PLAY! PLAY DOUGH

Bruna Assis Brasil/Arquivo da editora

FRUIT

1 LOOK, LISTEN AND SAY. 21

Ari Nicolosi/Arquivo da editora

DATE ..../........./.........

2 LISTEN AND CIRCLE.

Ari Nicolosi/Arquivo da editora

DATE ____ / ____ / ____

3 COLOR THE FRUITS.

④ MATCH.

Sittipong mangkon/Shutterstock

PaulPaladin/Shutterstock

YUTTASAK SAMPACHANO/Shutterstock

Tanya-Tinya/Shutterstock

PixaHub/Shutterstock

Kyselova Inna/Shutterstock

Anna Zheludkova/Shutterstock

Ihor L/Shutterstock

Pixel-Shot/Shutterstock

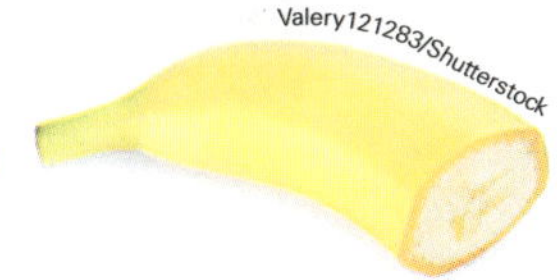

Valery121283/Shutterstock

DATE ..../......./.......

(5) LOOK AND NUMBER.

Fernando Favoretto/Criar Imagem

Ramon Espelt Photography/Shutterstock

Eising Studio - Food Photo & Video/Bon Appetit/Fotoarena

HelloRF Zcool/Shutterstock

DATE ____/____/____

LET'S SING! 22

FRUIT IS GOOD FOR YOU!

I LIKE FRUITS.
THEY ARE SO GOOD!
DO YOU LIKE FRUIT?
YES! IT IS GOOD FOOD!
I WANT APPLES.
I WANT ORANGES.
I WANT BANANAS.
I WANT FRUIT!

Fabiana Salomão/Arquivo da editora

DATE ____/____/____

LESSON 11

BREAKFAST

1 LOOK, LISTEN AND SAY. 23

DATE ....../....../......

② FIND 3 DIFFERENCES.

DATE ____ / ____ / ____

3 DRAW.

DATE ___/___/___

4 CIRCLE THE ODD ONE OUT.

Ilustrações: Ari Nicolosi/Arquivo da editora

Lightkite/Shutterstock

freesoulproduction/Shutterstock

Ari Nicolosi/Arquivo da editora

Ari Nicolosi/Arquivo da editora

Ilustrações: Ari Nicolosi/Arquivo da editora

DATE ____ / ____ / ____

5 DOT TO DOT AND COLOR.

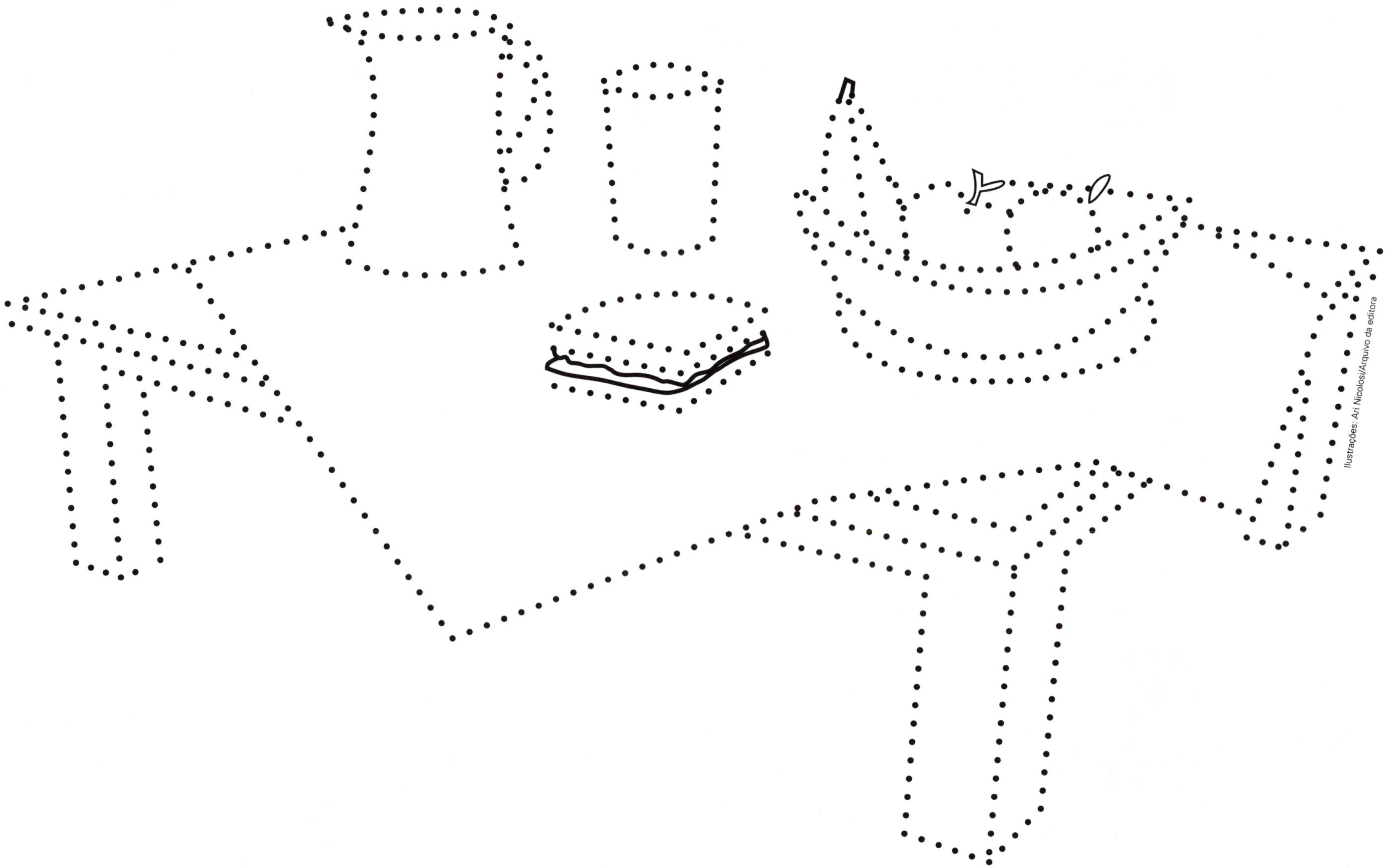

Ilustrações: Ari Nicolosi/Arquivo da editora

LET'S SING! 24

IT IS SNACK TIME!

IT IS SNACK TIME,
HURRAY! HURRAY!
MILK AND COOKIES,
MILK AND COOKIES.
I LIKE MILK,
I LIKE COOKIES,
IT IS SNACK TIME.
A DELICIOUS TIME!

Ilustrações: Ari Nicolosi/Arquivo da editora

DATE ___/___/___

LESSON 12

SET THE TABLE

1 LOOK, LISTEN AND SAY. 25

Ilustrações: Ari Nicolosi/Arquivo da editora

DATE .... / .... / ....

2 CIRCLE.

Ilustrações: Ari Nicolosi/Arquivo da editora

Ilustrações: Ari Nicolosi/Arquivo da editora

DATE ...... / ...... / ......

3 STICK.

Ari Nicolosi/Arquivo da editora

DATE ____ / ____ / ____

4 DRAW THE SEQUENCE.

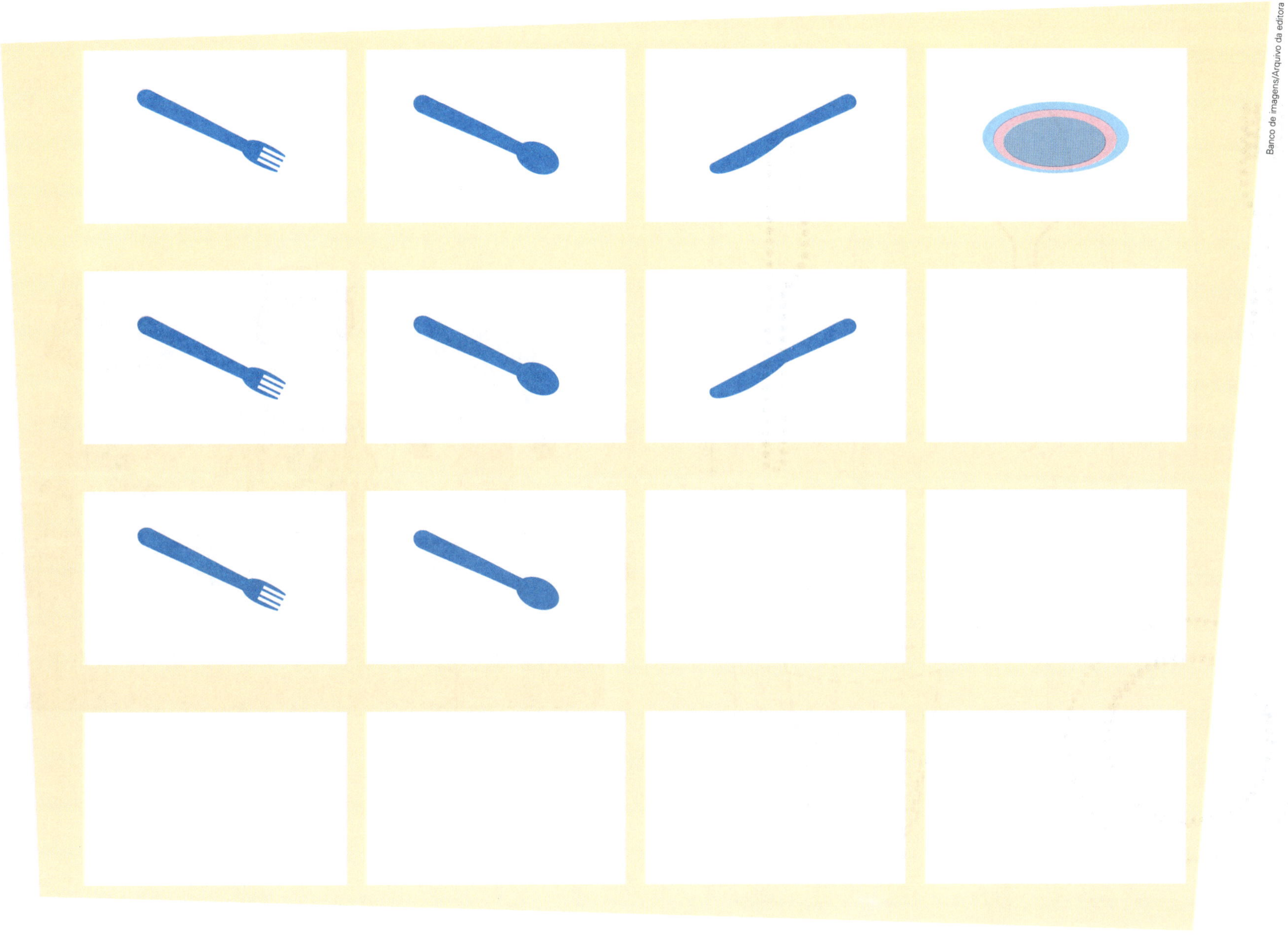

Banco de imagens/Arquivo da editora

DATE .... / .... / ....

5 DOT TO DOT AND CIRCLE.

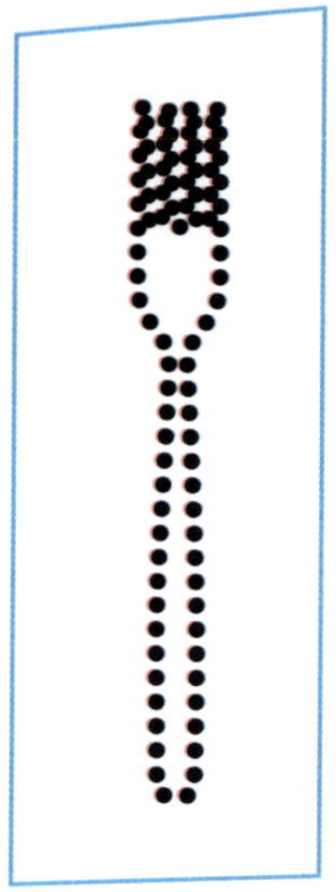
Creative icon styles/Shutterstock

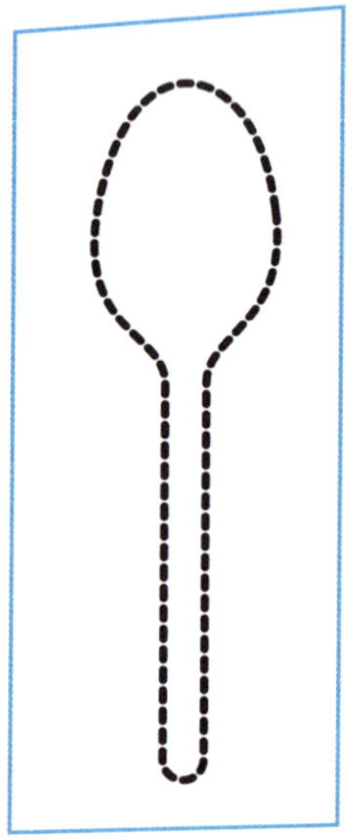
gst/Shutterstock

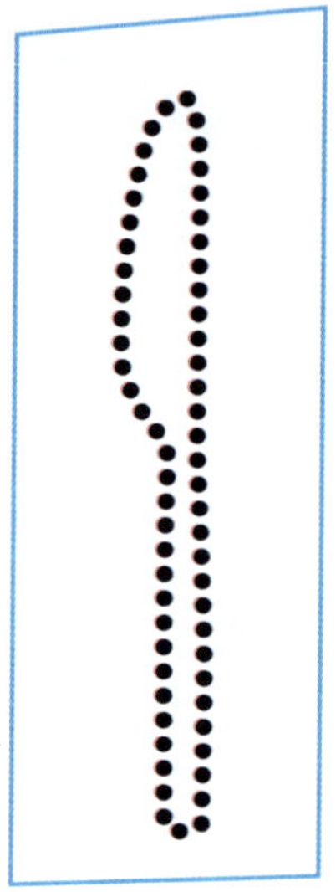
Creative icon styles/Shutterstock

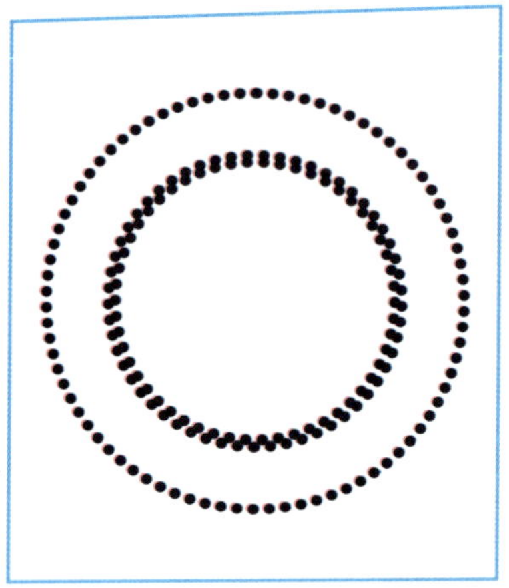
Creative icon styles/Shutterstock

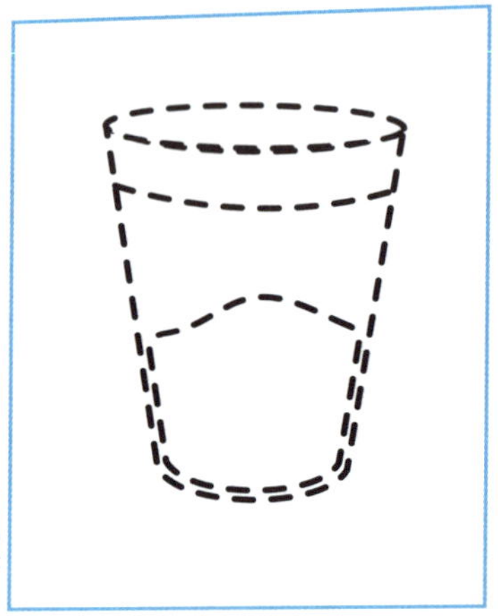
Giuseppe_R/Shutterstock

GraphicsRF/Shutterstock

LET'S SING! 26

SET THE TABLE

LET'S SET THE TABLE!
LET'S SET THE TABLE!
SPOON, FORK, KNIFE,
GLASS AND PLATE!
LET'S SET THE TABLE!
LET'S SET THE TABLE!

DATE ____/____/____

IT'S YOUR TURN!

LET'S MAKE A HEALTHY FOOD CATALOG!

1. LOOK AND SAY.

Africa Studio/Shutterstock

Rawpixel.com/Shutterstock

2. DRAW.

DATE ...... / ...... / ......

GLOSSARY

UNIT 1

BIRD

Litvalifa/Shutterstock

CAT

Litvalifa/Shutterstock

CHICK

Litvalifa/Shutterstock

CHICKEN

Litvalifa/Shutterstock

COW

Nerthuz/Shutterstock

CROCODILE

kongsky/Shutterstock

DOG

5 second Studio/ Shutterstock

DUCK

Litvalifa/Shutterstock

FARM

Golmer/Shutterstock

FISH

NooMUboN Photo/ Shutterstock

FLOWER

5 second Studio/ Shutterstock

HORSE

GeptaYs/Shutterstock

PET

VK Studio/Shutterstock

PIG

Tsekhmister/ Shutterstock

SUN

Surasak_Photo/Shutterstock

TREE

Tridsanu Thopet/Shutterstock

UNIT 2

BIKE

anetta/Shutterstock

BLUE

Luxury_Studio/Shutterstock

BOAT

Vereshchagin Dmitry/Shutterstock

BUS

InfantryDavid/Shutterstock

CAR

risteski goce/Shutterstock

GREEN

VF/Shutterstock

HOSPITAL

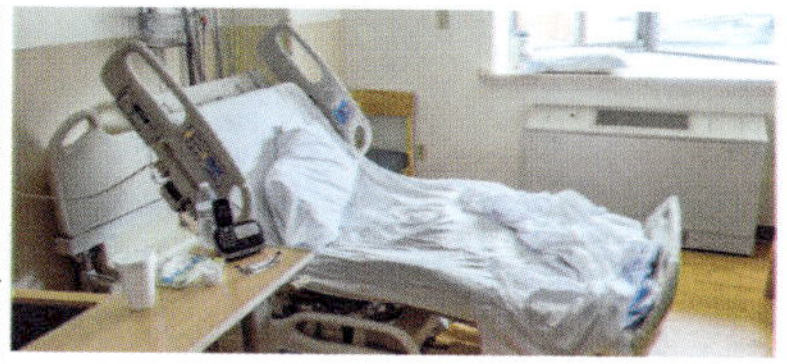
Christopher Sciacca/Shutterstock

ORANGE

Ksenia Stash/Shutterstock

PET SHOP

SariMe/Shutterstock

PINK

nani888/Shutterstock

PLANE

next143/Shutterstock

RED

Le Panda/Shutterstock

SCHOOL

ChiccoDodiFC/Shutterstoc

SUPERMARKET

Robert Kneschke/Shutterstock

YELLOW

nani888/Shutterstock

ONE
1

TWO
2

THREE
3

FOUR
4

FIVE
5

SIX
6

SEVEN
7

EIGHT
8

NINE
9

TEN
10

UNIT 3

BELLY

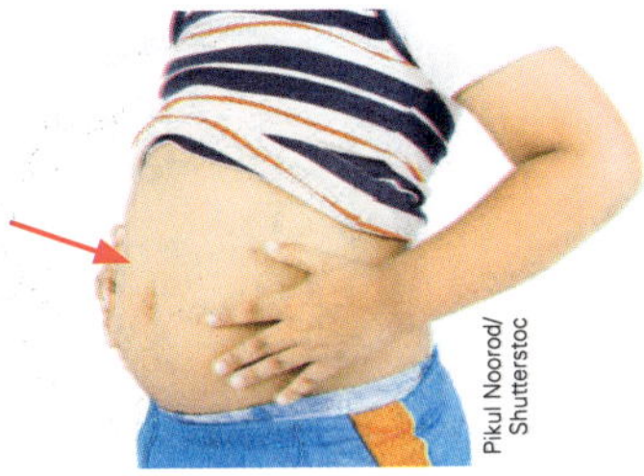

Pikul Noorod/ Shutterstoc

BRUSH YOUR TEETH

wavebreakmedia/Shutterstock

CAP

Etaphop photo/Shutterstock

COMB YOUR HAIR

all_about_people/Shutterstock

EAR

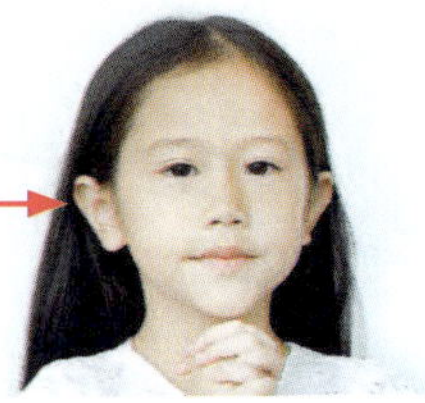

GOLFX/Shutterstock

EYE

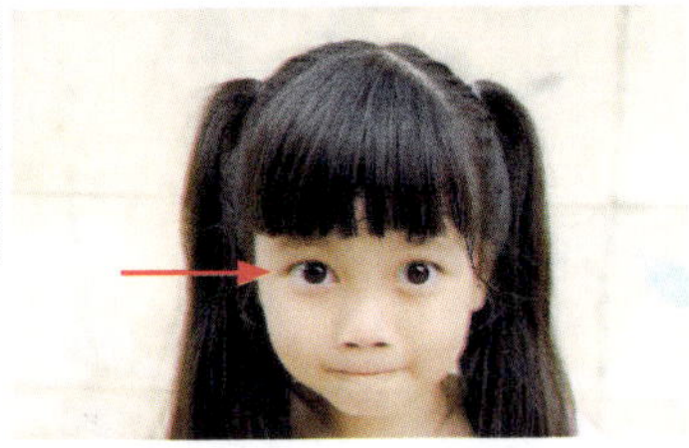

nalinda117/Shutterstock

FOOT

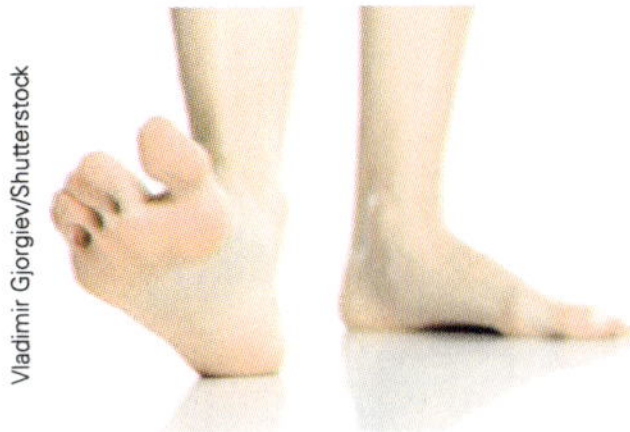

Vladimir Gjorgiev/Shutterstock

HAND

vayno/Shutterstock

HEAD

Samuel Borges Photography/Shutterstock

MOUTH

Bilanol/Shutterstock

NOSE

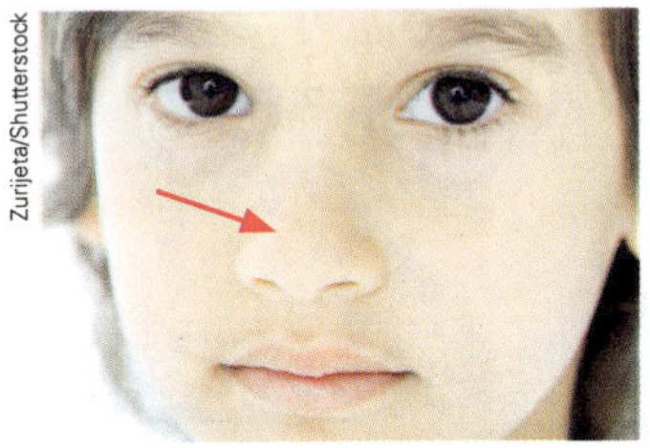

Zurijeta/Shutterstock

PANTS SHORTS

Pixel-Shot/Shutterstock

SNEAKERS

cypopcolour/Shutterstock

TAKE A SHOWER

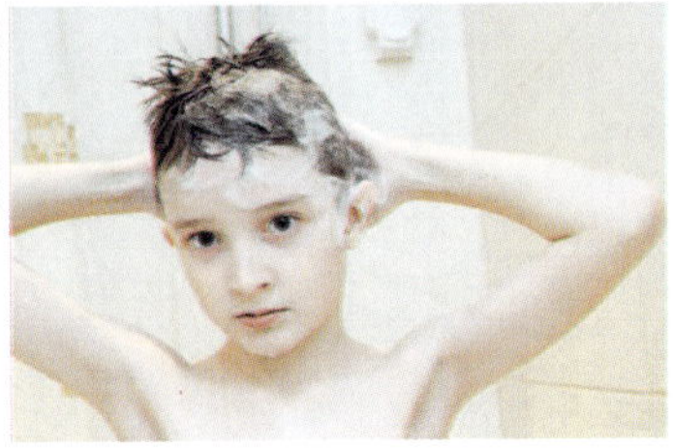

ReaLiia/Shutterstock

T-SHIRT

Ruslan Kudrin/ Shutterstock

WASH YOUR HANDS

noophoto/Shutterstock

UNIT 4

APPLE

Suggy/Shutterstoc

BANANA

StockerTu/Shutterstock

BREAD

Julian Weber/Shutterstock

COOKIES

New Africa/Shutterstock

CRACKERS

HelloRF Zcool/Shutterstock

FORK

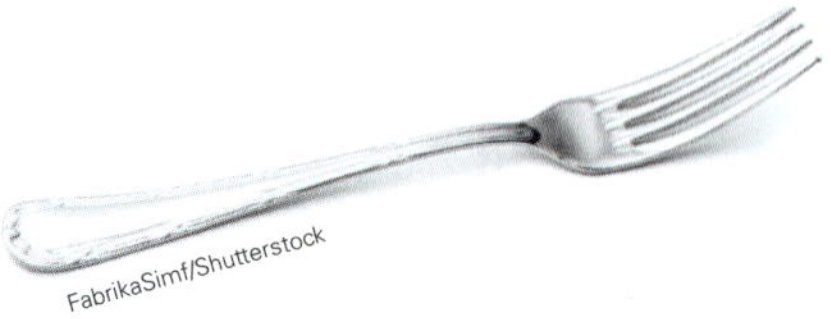

FabrikaSimf/Shutterstock

GLASS

Mira/Shutterstock

KNIFE

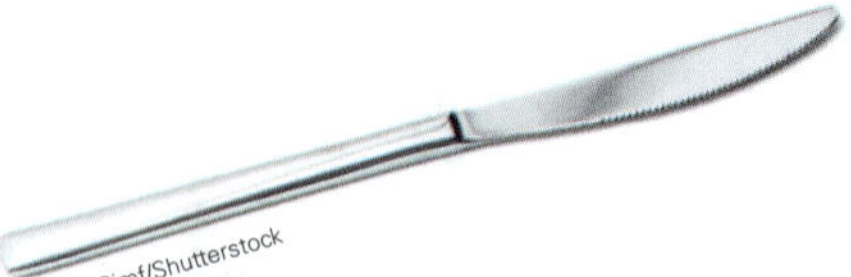

FabrikaSimf/Shutterstock

MILK

phive/Shutterstock

ORANGE ORANGE JUICE

Yegor Larin/Shutterstock

PAPAYA

Hong Vo/Shutterstock

PEAR

ilovezion/Shutterstock

PLATE

Kastaprav/Shutterstock

SANDWICH

New Africa/Shutterstock

SPOON

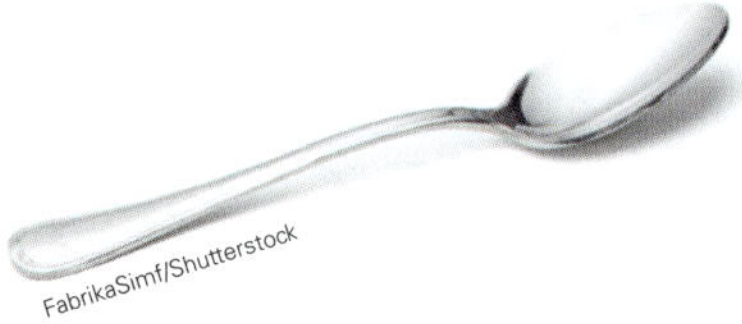

FabrikaSimf/Shutterstock

TABLE

Seyfettin Karagunduz/Shutterstock

Studio_G/Shutterstock

Helga Chirk/Shutterstock

inuinui studio/Shutterstock

THANKS FOR...

FROM: ....

TO: ....

MERRY CHRISTMAS
AND
HAPPY NEW YEAR!

FROM: ....

TO: ....

HAPPY
EASTER!

FROM: ....

TO: ....

MARCHA CRIANÇA

EDUCAÇÃO INFANTIL
LÍNGUA INGLESA 2

MEMORY GAME AND DOMINOES

editora scipione

Parte integrante da coleção Marcha Criança – Língua Inglesa – Educação Infantil

NAME: ....

CLASS: ....

GLUE
FOLD
FOLD
GLUE

MEMORY GAME

COW

COW

HORSE

HORSE

CHICKEN

CHICKEN

PIG

PIG

FISH

FISH

CAT

CAT

DOG

DOG

BIRD

BIRD

Ilustrações: Ari Nicolosi/Arquivo da editora

DOMINOES

Ilustrações: Ari Nicolosi, Ana Carolina Nitto/Arquivo da editora

STIC

PAGE 16

MARCHA CRIANÇA

LET'S MAKE POPCORN

ELIETE CANESI MORINO
RITA BRUGIN DE FARIA
ILUSTRAÇÕES DE ARI NICOLOSI

editora scipione

PAGE 60